DATE DUE
Fecha Para Retorna

GEOLOGY GENIUS
GEMSTONES

by Rebecca Pettiford

pogo

Ideas for Parents and Teachers

Pogo Books let children practice reading informational text while introducing them to nonfiction features such as headings, labels, sidebars, maps, and diagrams, as well as a table of contents, glossary, and index.

Carefully leveled text with a strong photo match offers early fluent readers the support they need to succeed.

Before Reading

- "Walk" through the book and point out the various nonfiction features. Ask the student what purpose each feature serves.
- Look at the glossary together. Read and discuss the words.

Read the Book

- Have the child read the book independently.
- Invite him or her to list questions that arise from reading.

After Reading

- Discuss the child's questions. Talk about how he or she might find answers to those questions.
- Prompt the child to think more. Ask: What did you know about gemstones before you read this book? What else would you like to learn?

Pogo Books are published by Jump!
5357 Penn Avenue South
Minneapolis, MN 55419
www.jumplibrary.com

Library of Congress Cataloging-in-Publication Data

Names: Pettiford, Rebecca, author.
Title: Gemstones / by Rebecca Pettiford.
Description: Minneapolis, MN : Jump!, Inc., [2018]
Series: Geology genius
"Pogo Books are published by Jump!"
Audience: Ages 7-10.
Includes bibliographical references and index.
Identifiers: LCCN 2017049616 (print)
LCCN 2017048794 (ebook)
ISBN 9781624968327 (ebook)
ISBN 9781624968303 (hardcover : alk. paper)
ISBN 9781624968310 (pbk.)
Subjects: LCSH: Precious stones–Juvenile literature.
Classification: LCC QE392.2 (print)
LCC QE392.2 .P485 2018 (ebook) | DDC 553.8–dc23
LC record available at https://lccn.loc.gov/2017049616

Editor: Kristine Spanier
Book Designers: Molly Ballanger & Leah Sanders
Content Consultant: Sandra Feher, M.S.G.E.

Photo Credits: All photos by Shutterstock except: malerapaso/iStock, cover; Stephen Chung/Alamy, 1; alicenerr/123RF, 8; National Gem Collection, National Museum of Natural History/Smithsonian, 9; Phillippe Gouvela/iStock, 14-15; Tooga/Getty, 16; www.timfisherphotos.com/Getty, 17, Eugen Wais/Alamy; 20-21; PATRICK KOVARIK/Getty, 23.

Printed in the United States of America at Corporate Graphics in North Mankato, Minnesota.

TABLE OF CONTENTS

CHAPTER 1

WHAT ARE GEMSTONES?

Throughout history, gemstones have been a sign of wealth. Why? They are **rare**. They are valuable. The crowns of royalty are often covered in them.

Where do they come from? Most come from **crystals** in **minerals**. They are **mined** from Earth's surface. They are mined beneath it, too. They are cut and polished into shiny gems.

Some gems come from plants and animals. Pearls are gems made by oysters. How? Sand and other material get inside the shell. The materials are coated with a special substance. Finally, a pearl forms. Clams and other shellfish make pearls, too.

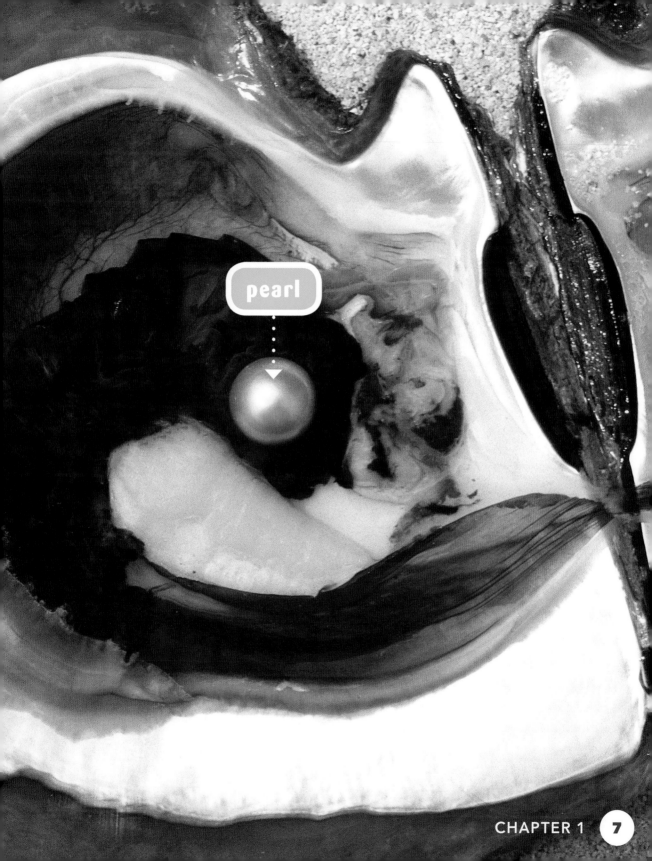

pearl

CHAPTER 2

RARE BEAUTY

Gems are rare. They are hard to mine. This is why they cost a lot. A stone's value is also determined by its size.

diamond mine

Gems are measured in **carats**. One carat is 0.2 grams (.007 ounces).

The Hope Diamond is more than 45 carats in size! Some say it is worth 350 million dollars.

Hope Diamond

Every stone has a set of physical features. **Luster** describes how shiny a stone is. It is the way light reflects from its surface.

Gems come in many colors. Red. Orange. Yellow. Green. Blue. Violet. Why are they different colors? Their color depends on the way they draw in light.

TAKE A LOOK!

White light is made of all the colors of the rainbow. A gem acts like a prism. When light strikes it, some of these colors are drawn in. Others are not. Instead, they are reflected back. These are the colors you see when you look at a stone.

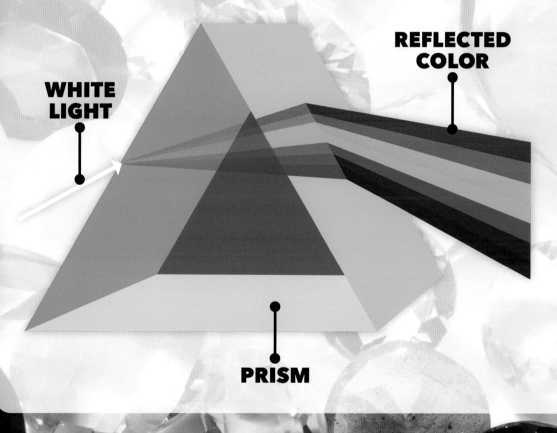

WHITE LIGHT

REFLECTED COLOR

PRISM

Hardness describes how easy it is to scratch a stone. The Mohs scale gives a number to a stone's hardness. A diamond is the hardest. It is a ten.

Amber is soft. It is a two. Amber is ancient tree **resin**. Some early plants and animals have been trapped in it.

amber

CHAPTER 3

MAKING THE CUT

Why do gemstones come in different shapes?

Gem cutters use hard stones to cut softer stones. They cut the surfaces into a number of flat faces. These are called **facets**. They give a stone its final shape.

birthstone

Some people give **birthstones** as gifts. Each month has its own stones. Some people like to wear them in jewelry.

TAKE A LOOK!

Some months have more than one birthstone. The gems shown are the most popular. What is your birthstone?

GARNET
January

AMETHYST
February

AQUAMARINE
March

DIAMOND
April

EMERALD
May

PEARL
June

RUBY
July

PERIDOT
August

SAPPHIRE
September

TOURMALINE
October

TOPAZ
November

BLUE TOPAZ
December

crown of
King Louis XV
of France

Would you like to see large, valuable gemstones up close? Visit a museum. Some of the world's most beautiful gemstones are on display. Everyone can enjoy them. Including you!

DID YOU KNOW?

Gems are found in museums all around the world. The crown of King Louis XV is in the Louvre Museum in France.

ACTIVITIES & TOOLS

POLISH YOUR ROCKS

All stones look better when they are polished. It brings out their natural beauty. Build a rock tumbler for your collection.

What You Need:
- small stones
- tall plastic container with lid
- water
- sand

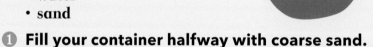

❶ Fill your container halfway with coarse sand.

❷ Pour water into the container so that $2/3$ of the container is filled. Mix water and sand to form a slurry.

❸ Put your stones into the slurry. Cover the container with its lid. Use duct tape to cover the mouth of the container if the lid is loose.

❹ Shake and roll the tumbler in all directions. Repeat for several days.

Your stones started out with rough edges. It may take a month or longer for them to become smooth. To help the process, replace the coarse sand with fine sand. This will help polish your rocks even more.

GLOSSARY

birthstones: Gemstones that are associated with the month of a person's birthday.

carats: Units for measuring the weight of gemstones.

crystals: Repeating, three-dimensional arrangements of atoms or molecules.

facets: The flat, polished surfaces of cut gems.

fossilized: Something that has changed into a fossil; a fossil is the remains, a trace, or print of a plant or animal from the past that is preserved in rock.

luster: The way light reflects from the surface of a gem.

mined: Dug from a pit or tunnel.

minerals: Solid, natural substances with crystal structures, usually obtained from the ground.

rare: Not often seen or found.

resin: A yellow or brown sticky substance that comes from some trees.

sediment: Minerals, mud, gravel, or sand, or a combination of these, that have been carried to a place by water, wind, or glaciers.

synthetic: Manufactured or artificial.

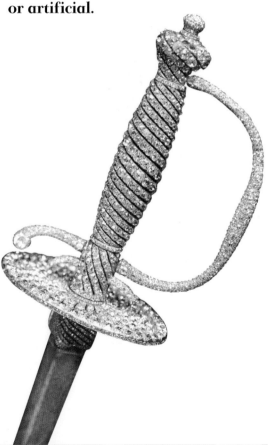

INDEX

TO LEARN MORE

Learning more is as easy as 1, 2, 3.

1) Go to www.factsurfer.com

2) Enter "gemstones" into the search box.

3) Click the "Surf" button to see a list of websites.

With factsurfer, finding more information is just a click away.